John Gay's
Book of Cats

John Gay's Book of Cats

DAVID & CHARLES

Newton Abbot London Vancouver

0 7153 6696 3

Set in 11 on 12 Garamond and printed in
Great Britain by Ebenezer Baylis & Son Limited,
The Trinity Press, Worcester, and London
for David & Charles (Holdings) Limited
South Devon House Newton Abbot Devon

Published in Canada
by Douglas David & Charles Limited
132 Philip Avenue North Vancouver BC

Stevie Smith's poem The Galloping Cat *(pages 20-21) is reproduced by permission
of her executor, James MacGibbon*

Contents

Introduction

You will almost certainly have seen many of John Gay's photographs—in advertising, in other books and so on—without of course knowing who the photographer was or anything about him. (He has in fact published two books, one of them in collaboration with Sir John Betjeman, and had at least one photograph in every number of a distinguished magazine of the countryside.) But if you are interested in cats it is also pretty certain that it was precisely John Gay's pictures that most arrested your attention and kept you looking at them longer than average. Because John Gay brings an extra quality to his work. He is not only a superb artist and technician but a genuine cat enthusiast, understanding them, loving them, laughing with them rather than at them, being infuriated with them, but always respecting their dignity. 'Dogs look up to you, cats look down and pigs is equal.'

He takes a great deal of trouble to find the right cat for the setting of one of his pictures and then he spends time getting to know the cat or, more important, letting the cat get to know him. 'The cat has to make the first move.' He waits patiently while the cat explores natural and sometimes unnatural surroundings so that eventually he can capture an expression or antic that is characteristic and so easily recognisable by those with a cat of the same kind in the family.

He finds his subjects among derelict buildings, in shops, in the street and at the homes of friends and acquaintances. He captures with his camera those crouched ready to spring on unsuspecting prey, lazing in the sun, mothering their young or staring disinterestedly at nothing in particular. And knowing the insatiable curiosity of the cat he photographs its reaction to movement, and unfamiliar object, sound or situation. As one might perhaps expect he has strong personal preferences. 'Give me an alley cat every time,' he says. But though the aristocratic pure breeds may generally be less rewarding to work with, some have their place here and indeed one such of John Gay's clients is probably the best known cat in the advertising world.

This then is not just another cat book. Indeed, as a cat lover I have always wanted a cat picture book to be linked with in England and America, but a book that was genuinely different and better. Here after sifting through literally thousands of John Gay's pictures we have it. I hope it gives you as much satisfaction as it has and will continue to give me.

David St John Thomas

1 Mothering Cats and Kittens

Wash your hands and pray   Kipling *The Glory of the Garden*

mewing her mighty youth, and kindling
her undazzled eyes at the full midday beam
Milton *Areopagitica*

The child that is not clean and neat,
With lots of toys and things to eat,
He is a naughty child, I'm sure—
Or else his dear papa is poor.
R L Stevenson *The Land of the Counterpane*

2 Curious Cats

The Galloping Cat *by Stevie Smith*

Oh I am a cat that likes to
Gallop about doing good
So
One day when I was
Galloping about doing good, I saw
A Figure in the path; I said:
Get off! (Be-
cause
I am a cat that likes to
Gallop about doing good)
But he did not move, instead
He raised his hand as if
To land me a cuff
So I made to dodge so as to
Prevent him bringing it orf,
Un-for-tune-ately I slid

Some Ass had left instead
Of putting in the bin. So
His hand caught me on the cheek
I tried
To lay his arm open from wrist to elbow
With my sharp teeth
Because I am
A cat that likes to gallop about doing good
Would you believe it?
He wasn't there
My teeth met nothing but air,
But a Voice said: Poor cat,
(Meaning me) and a soft stroke
Came on me head
Since when
I have been bald.

Also I heard a swoosh
As of wings, and saw
A halo shining at the height of
Mrs Gubbins's backyard fence,
So I thought: What's the good
Of galloping about doing good
When angels stand in the path
And do not do as they should
Such as having an arm to be bitten off
All the same I
Intend to go on being
A cat that likes to
Gallop about doing good
So
Now with my bald head I go,
Chopping the untidy flowers down, to
  and fro,

An' scooping up the grass to show
Underneath
The cinder path of wrath
Ha ha ha ha, ho,
Angels aren't the only ones who do not know
What's what and that
Galloping about doing good
Is a full-time job
That needs
An experienced eye of earthly
Sharpness, worth I dare say
(If you'll forgive a personal note)
A good deal more
Than all that skyey stuff
Of angels that make so bold as
To.pity a cat like me that
Gallops about doing good.

3 On Guard

Folks *prefer* in fact a hovel to your dreary marble halls

Dogs look up at you, cats look down, and pigs is equal
Anon

I am tall and rather stately,
And I care not very greatly
What you say, or what you do.

I am monarch of all I survey,
My right there is none to dispute

Property has its duties
as well as its rights

4 The Hunter

Thou shalt not be afraid for any terror by night
The Book of Common Prayer

Beware the fury of a
patient man
Dryden *Absalom and Achitophel*

If 'men are suspicious',
so are cats
Herrick

30

5 Cat and Dog

Animals are such agreeable friends—they ask no questions, they
pass no criticisms   George Eliot *Mr Gilfil's Love-Story*

The more I see of men, the better I like dogs

Merely innocent flirtation,
Not quite adultery, but adulteration
Byron *Don Juan*

6 Meddling, Mischievous Cats

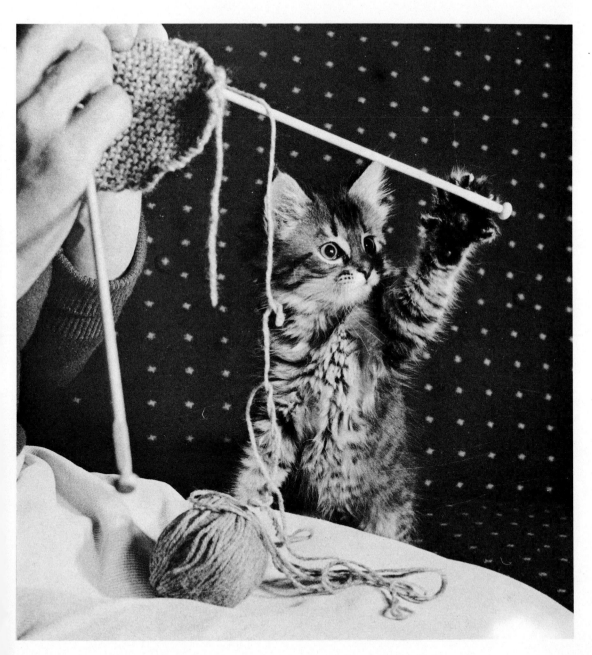

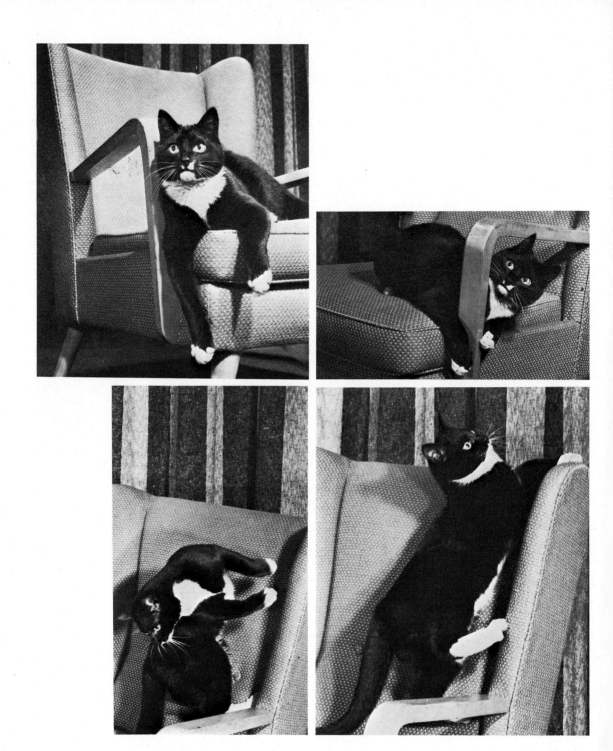

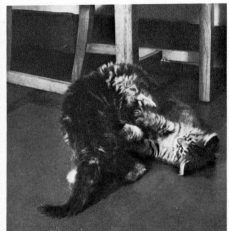

7 Cats Always Find the Most Comfortable Spot

I slept, and dreamed that life was Beauty;
I woke and found that life was Duty
Ellen Sturgis Hooper *Life a Duty*

This warm kind world is all I know
William Johnson Cory *Mimnermus in Church*

8 In Trade and Profession

Some books are to be tasted, others to be swallowed, and some few to be chewed and digested
Francis Bacon

By their fruits ye shall know them
Bible (St Matthew VII v 20)

His best companions,
innocence and health
Goldsmith *The Deserted Village*

Cookery is become an art, a noble science; cooks are gentlemen
Robert Burton (1577–1640)

9 Everyday, Everywhere Cats

Though I am always in haste,
I am never in a hurry
John Wesley *Select Letters*

Your wheel is new and your pumps are strange, But otherwise I perceive no change
Kipling *A Truthful Song*

10 Very Superior Cats

As Orwell and others have
said, 'All animals are equal,
but some animals are more
equal than others'.

My name is George Nathaniel Curzon, I am a most superior person

11 Contented Cats

Let the curtains fall. . . . So
let us welcome peaceful
ev'ning in.
Cowper *The Winter Evening*